Brain

Injury, Illness, and Health

Revised and updated

Steve Parker

**Heinemann Library,
Chicago, Illinois**

www.heinemannraintree.com
Visit our website to find out
more information about
Heinemann-Raintree books.

To order:
☎ Phone 888-454-2279
🖳 Visit www.heinemannraintree.com
to browse our catalog and order online.

Edited by Andrew Farrow, Adrian Vigliano, and
  Pollyanna Poulter
Designed by Steven Mead and Geoff Ward
Original illustrations © Capstone Global Library Limited 2003
Illustrated by David Woodroffe and Geoff Ward
Picture research by Ruth Blair
Originated by Heinemann Library
Printed and bound in China by CTPS

13 12 11 10 09
10 9 8 7 6 5 4 3 2 1

Second edition ISBNs: 978 1 4329 3410 1 (hardcover)
                      978 1 4329 3423 1 (paperback)

**The Library of Congress has cataloged the first edition
as follows:**
Parker, Steve.
  Brain / Steve Parker.
    p. cm. -- (Body focus : injury, illness and health)
  Includes bibliographical references and index.
  Contents: Introducing the brain -- Main brain parts -- Blood
for the brain -- Brain and head injury -- The brain's building
blocks -- How brain cells 'talk'-- The brainstem -- The body's
monitor -- Emotions and the body clock -- The sleeping brain
-- Cerebellum and movement -- The brain's nerves -- The
cerebral cortex -- Two sides of the brain -- At the center
of the brain -- Brain infections -- Brain disorders -- Brain
development -- The brain in the future.
    ISBN 1-4034-0748-7 (lib. bdg.) -- ISBN 1-4034-3296-1
(pbk.)
    1. Brain--Juvenile literature. 2. Neurophysiology--Juvenile
literature. 3. Brain--Diseases--Juvenile literature.   [1. Brain.]
  I. Title. II. Series: Body focus.
  QP376.P347 2003
  612.8'2--dc21
                        2002152948

Acknowledgments
The author and publishers are grateful to the following for
permission to reproduce copyright material: Action Plus p. **27**;
Alamy p. **24**; Corbis pp. **13** (Todd Gipstein), **22** (Michael Cole),
31 (moodboard), **41**; Getty Images pp. **9** (Steve Dunwell), **11**,
17, **21**; John Walmsley p. **28**; Photolibrary pp. **4** and **19** (Age
Footstock), **33** (Index Stock Imagery); Science Photo Library
pp. **10** and **15** (CNRI), **5**, **7** (Scott Camazine), **12** (Alfred
Pasieka), **32** (Montreal Neuro Institute), **35**, **36** (Sinclair
Stammers), **37** (Dr. P Marazzi), **38**, **39** (Gca/CNRI), **40** (Petit
Format/ Nestlé), **42** (Simon Fraser), **43** (James King-Holmes).

Cover photograph of a CT brain scan reproduced with
permission of Science Photo Library (Pasieka).

We would like to thank David Wright for his invaluable
help in the preparation of this book.

Every effort has been made to contact copyright holders
of material reproduced in this book. Any omissions will
be rectified in subsequent printings if notice is given to
the publisher.

Disclaimer
All the Internet addresses (URLs) given in this book were valid
at the time of going to press. However, due to the dynamic
nature of the Internet, some addresses may have changed, or
sites may have changed or ceased to exist since publication.
While the author and publisher regret any inconvenience this
may cause readers, no responsibility for any such changes can
be accepted by either the author or the publisher.

Contents

Words appearing in the text in bold, **like this**, are explained in the glossary.

Introducing
the Brain

The human body is made up of many different parts, including the liver, kidneys, stomach, intestines, brain, bones, muscles, and heart. Each part works independently, but all the parts work together in a coordinated manner so that the body as a whole can function and be healthy. The main system specialized for the control and coordination of all body parts is the nervous system. Its most important part is the brain. The brain receives information from outside the body, from the eyes, ears, and other sense organs. It also decides which movements and actions we make, and it controls the muscles used to carry these out.

Brain and mind

The brain is the site of the human mind. It is where we think, have ideas, feel emotions, change moods, express desires, solve problems, and store and recall memories. These are known as higher **mental** processes. We are aware of them in our minds.

There are also many other processes that the brain carries out, but that we are not usually aware of. Examples of these include controlling the heartbeat, breathing, and digestion. These are known as lower-level processes. We do not have to think about making them happen. They are part of the "automatic brain."

 Playing fast-action video and computer games may not involve much physical activity, but it gives the brain a real workout.

Brain trouble

The brain is so complicated, and also so important as the body's control center, that problems affecting it can have far-reaching effects. Some of these problems have a physical cause, which we can detect and describe. This makes them easier to understand. For example, a bang on the head can cause a person to be "knocked out," or lose consciousness, as the brain is suddenly shaken and bruised inside the skull.

Other brain problems seem to have no obvious cause. An example is the condition of epilepsy, when a kind of "electrical storm" in the brain can bring on a seizure (see page 39). Lack of a clear cause may make these brain conditions more difficult to understand, yet they can have far-reaching effects on a person's life.

The medical study of the brain, spinal cord, nerves, and the disorders that affect them is known as neurology. The study of the mind, and how we think and behave, is known as psychology.

More knowledge

Brain scientists often say that we have learned more about the brain in the past 10 years than in all the years and centuries before. This increasing amount of knowledge continues, week by week, year by year. It is now helping to unravel some of the brain's great secrets, such as how memories form and the puzzle of **consciousness**.

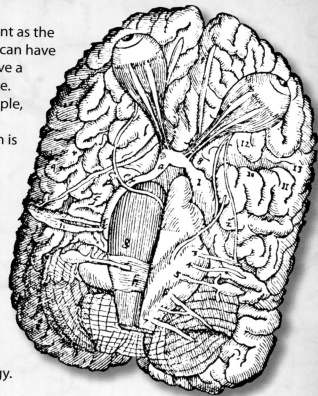

Old diagrams of the brain look strange and outdated today. Will today's diagrams seem strange and outdated in the future?

(see page 39)

IN FOCUS: THE NERVOUS SYSTEM

The body's nervous system has three main parts:

- The central nervous system (CNS) consists of the brain and spinal cord.

- The **peripheral** nervous system (PNS) includes the network of nerves that carry messages between various parts of the body and the brain and spinal cord.

- The **autonomic** nervous system (ANS) has parts in both the CNS and PNS. It deals with autonomic (or "automatic") body processes, such as digestion, breathing, and heart rate.

Main Parts of the Brain

The average adult human brain weighs about 1,400 grams (49 ounces). It is pinkish-gray in color, feels like stiff gelatin, and is covered with deep, wrinkle-like grooves. The brain has four major parts: the **cerebrum**, cerebellum, diencephalon, and brain stem.

Cerebrum

The cerebrum makes up about seven-eighths of the brain. It is the large, wrinkled "lump" that curves over and covers most of the other parts of the brain. It is the main site of consciousness, ideas, feelings, and memories—it is the "thinking" part of the brain.

The cerebrum has two parts, or halves, known as the left and right cerebral hemispheres. These are separated by a deep groove. Each hemisphere has an outer, gray-colored, wrinkled layer, called the cerebral **cortex**. The two halves are joined by a long strip, the corpus callosum, that carries nerve signals between them.

Cerebellum

At the lower rear of the brain is the cerebellum ("little brain"). With its rounded, wrinkled surface, it resembles a smaller version of the cerebrum. Its main task is to deal with nerve signals sent to the muscles. This allows the body to keep its balance and posture, and to make movements that are smooth, precise, and coordinated, rather than jerky and clumsy.

Diencephalon

The diencephalon is in the center of the brain, with the cerebrum above and the cerebellum behind. It includes the thalamus (see page 34) in the middle and the **hypothalamus** (see page 20) at the lower front. The diencephalon helps to alter our level of awareness, whether we are fully alert, drowsy, daydreaming, or even asleep. It also checks information coming from the eyes and other sense organs (except for the nose) and takes part in moods, emotions, and basic feelings, such as hunger, thirst, fear, and rage.

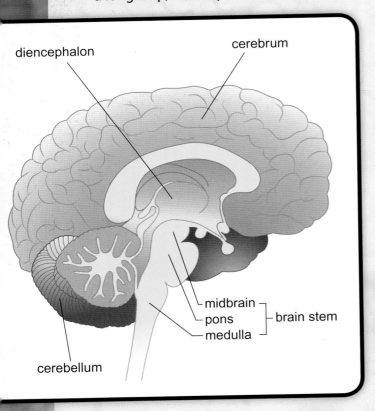

diencephalon

cerebrum

midbrain
pons — brain stem
medulla

cerebellum

The brain takes up the top half of the head. Its lower-rear parts extend down to the level of the mouth. It is protected inside the strong, dome-shaped skull bone.

Brain stem

The brain stem is the lowest part of the brain. At its base, it tapers downward and passes through a hole in the bottom of the skull. It then merges with the spinal cord, which is the body's main nerve.

The brain stem is the main "automatic" part of the brain. It deals with essential processes, such as heartbeat, breathing, and digestion, that we do not have to think about.

The energy-hungry brain

The brain seems still and unchanging. However, it is very busy at the microscopic level of body chemicals and electrical signals. Every second, trillions of nerve messages flash around inside it. This requires energy. The brain forms about one-fiftieth of the body's total weight, yet it uses more than one-tenth of the body's total energy.

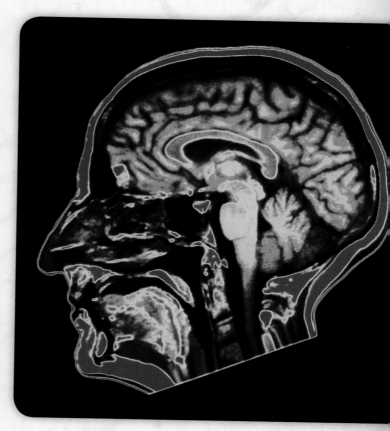

Modern medical scanners can show the living brain inside the head, and even pinpoint the parts that are working the most, based on the amounts of energy they are using.

HEALTH FOCUS: Keep up the "thinking energy"

The brain's need for a constant supply of energy can affect the way we think and concentrate. The body's energy comes from food. If we miss a meal, or eat the wrong type of food, this can reduce the energy supply. We may feel "light-headed" and unable to think clearly or to make fast, sensible decisions. In sports and activities, it is important to maintain the supply of energy, not only to the muscles, heart, and lungs, but also to the brain. The brain mainly uses glucose for energy.

Around the Brain

The brain is well protected by the hard, domed skull bones around it. It does not press up against the inside of the skull bone, but is separated by three sheet-like layers, or **membranes**, with fluid between. These layers are called the **meninges**. They wrap around the whole brain and also extend downward, around the spinal cord.

Fluid around the brain

There is a slight gap between the middle and inner meninges. This is called the subarachnoid space, and it contains a special liquid, known as cerebrospinal fluid, (CSF). The liquid forms a "pool" in which the brain floats, cushioning it from knocks and vibrations. (This fluid also fills the subarachnoid space around the spinal cord.)

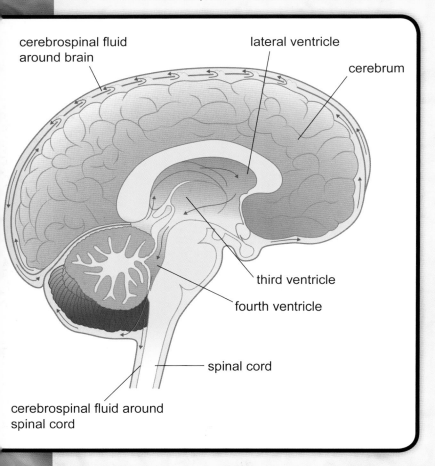

cerebrospinal fluid around brain

lateral ventricle

cerebrum

third ventricle

fourth ventricle

spinal cord

cerebrospinal fluid around spinal cord

Ventricles

Cerebrospinal fluid is present not only around the brain, but also inside it. There are four small chambers, or **ventricles**, inside the brain, linked by passageways. Two are called lateral ventricles, one in each cerebral hemisphere. The third ventricle is in the diencephalon, and the fourth is inside the brain stem.

Circulation of fluid

Cerebrospinal fluid is not still. It is made continuously by the linings of the ventricle chambers. It oozes in a slow, one-way flow, out of three small passageways from the fourth ventricle, into the subarachnoid space around the brain and spinal cord. It then seeps slowly through the meninges and is carried away by the blood. In this way, the cerebrospinal fluid collects and removes unwanted substances and wastes from around the brain.

 The brain is partly hollow, containing four chambers known as ventricles. These are filled with cerebrospinal fluid, which is made by parts of the ventricle lining. It flows slowly through small gaps, called apertures, out and around the brain and spinal cord.

A sample of brain fluid

To diagnose some health problems, a small sample of cerebrospinal fluid is taken for medical tests. It is usually withdrawn from the lower spinal cord using a long, hollow needle. This procedure is called lumbar puncture. Presence of blood in the fluid may indicate a leak of blood, or **hemorrhage**, around the brain, while certain germs can suggest an infection, such as meningitis.

HEALTH FOCUS: Added protection

The brain is perhaps the best-protected part of the body. It is surrounded by the layers and fluid of the meninges, and by the strong skull bones. Muscle, skin, and hair also protect the head, and some people wear a hat or a helmet for added protection. Even so, a bang on the head can cause great damage. Blows or knocks to the head are a risk in many sports and activities, from football to skiing and skateboarding. This is why helmets and other protective headgear are so important and, in many cases, required. A broken arm usually mends—but a damaged brain may not.

Hard hats or helmets are required by law at many hazardous areas, including construction and industrial sites.

Blood for the Brain

Most body parts have a simple blood supply. Blood arrives along a tube or **blood vessel** called an artery and is taken away along another vessel, called a vein. The brain is different. It has four arteries that bring blood up from the heart, through the neck, and into the skull. Two of these, the carotid arteries, carry blood mainly to the upper and front parts of the brain. The other two, the vertebral arteries, bring blood to the lower and rear parts of the brain.

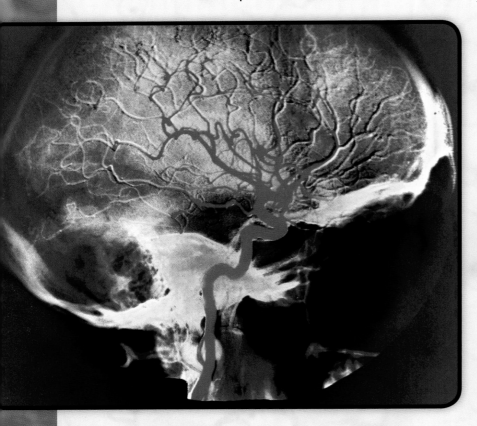

A cerebral angiogram or arteriogram is a specialized X-ray that shows the many branching blood vessels that supply the brain tissues with blood. Blockage of a vessel can cause the disorder known as a stroke.

A circular bypass

At the base of the brain, the four arteries are quite close to one another. They are joined or linked by extra arteries that form a "circle" under the brain. This is known as the cerebral arterial circle (circle of Willis). It is a kind of fail-safe design and means that if one artery is blocked or damaged, blood from the others can reach the parts of the brain it would normally supply.

The brain's veins

As blood leaves the brain, it does not flow straight into a vein. It oozes into pools, called dural sinuses, around the top of the brain. These come together at the lower rear of the brain and feed into two main veins, which carry blood out of the skull, back down through the neck, to the heart.

When blood supply fails

The brain suffers from a lack of blood faster than any other body part. The supply may fail for several reasons. This could include underlying blood vessel problems, such as narrowing and hardening of the arteries, or a blood clot swept along from elsewhere in the body.

Depending on the part of the brain that lacks blood, symptoms may include weakness, dizziness, headache, numbness, tingling, **paralysis** (loss of muscle control) that affects speech and movement, and loss of consciousness.

If a blockage quickly breaks up, and blood flow is restored, these symptoms fade. The condition is known as transient ischemic attack (TIA). (Ischemia is a lack of oxygen in the blood supply to a body part.) If the blood supply continues to fail, the result is a stroke. The symptoms and effects last longer, and some may be permanent.

HEALTH FOCUS: Strokes

In many industrialized regions, strokes cause up to one-third of all deaths and long-term disability. There are several reasons for this. They include smoking and an unhealthy diet, which both cause arteries to become narrowed and stiffened, increasing the risk of a blood clot. Lack of exercise, being overweight, and high blood pressure can also increase the risk of stroke. However, rapid medical treatment with "clot-buster" (thrombolytic) drugs, anti-platelet drugs (such as aspirin), or perhaps surgery, can reduce many of the immediate problems and also reduce the aftereffects.

A stroke can make it difficult for a person to walk or talk. But many forms of treatment and rehabilitation help a person to return to a normal life.

Brain and Head Injury

Despite the brain's various layers of protection, it can be damaged by a hard knock or crushing blow. There are several main types of damage, which have different effects, and various problems can take different times to develop. This is why it is important to seek expert medical advice for any kind of hard knock, jolt, or blow to the head or neck.

Bang on the brain

During a blow to the head, the brain may suffer a physical knock, especially on the cortex (surface) as it slams against the inside of the skull. This upsets the millions of delicate nerve messages and can cause minor bruising.

Sometimes the effects of a blow to the head are limited. For example, a knock on the lower rear of the skull may affect the visual cortex, or "vision center," which is the part of the brain in this region, just under the skull. The "vision center" deals with nerve messages from the eyes. The effect of the blow may be blurred or disturbed vision—what is often referred to as "seeing stars."

In some cases, a bang to the head causes the brain to shake back and forth, or "wobble," within the skull. This can affect many of its parts.

Concussion

A blow to the head may cause a person to lose consciousness. We call this a "knockout," "passing out," or a "blackout." Sometimes this happens for a few seconds, or perhaps a minute or two. The person then recovers consciousness and "comes to." This temporary, limited loss of consciousness is called a **concussion**. It may be followed by a period of feeling dazed, perhaps with memory loss, headache, muscle weakness, and numbness or tingling.

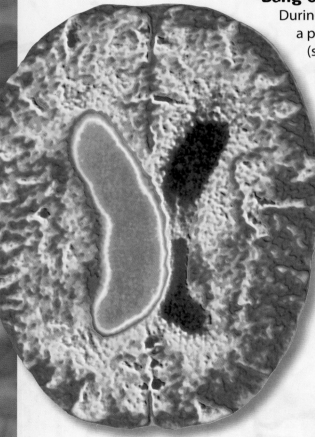

The red patch on the left side of this brain scan is a hematoma (pool of blood). It marks the site of a stroke, where blood vessels are damaged and leaking. This presses on the surrounding parts of the brain.

Bleeding

Another type of damage caused by a head injury is a leakage of blood, known as a hemorrhage, from a blood vessel. Blood seeping into the brain itself is called a cerebral hemorrhage. If outer vessels rupture, blood may leak around or between the meninges layers. This is loosely called a "brain hemorrhage," even though the blood is not actually in the brain.

Blood leaks may result, not only from head injury, but also from other conditions. One is an **aneurysm**, a weak region of an artery (blood vessel) wall. This can balloon outward and eventually split or rupture.

Pressure on the brain

In any of these cases, the leak may form a pool of blood, known as a hematoma. This cannot expand outward because of the rigid skull bone. So it presses inward, on the brain. The effects of this pressure include drowsiness, headache, confusion, nausea, numbness, weakness, paralysis, and, perhaps, long-term unconsciousness or coma.

 No matter how skilled the rider, a bicycle helmet can protect against head injury. In many sports, the rules insist that helmets be worn.

The Brain's Building Blocks

The brain, like other parts of the body, is made of trillions of microscopic "building blocks," known as **cells**. The main cells in the brain are nerve cells, or neurons—there are more than 100 billion of them. They are among the most long-lasting and specialized cells in the whole body. There are also cells that support and provide nourishment for the nerve cells, and take part in some kinds of nerve signaling. These are known as glial cells, and there are 10 times more of them than nerve cells.

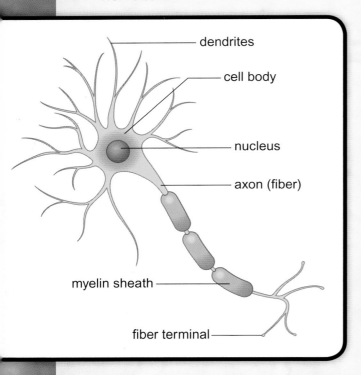

Long extensions called dendrites, and an even longer, thicker nerve fiber, or axon, spread from the main body of a nerve cell spread.

Features of a nerve cell

A typical nerve cell has three main parts.

- The **cell body** is much the same as other cells.
- **Dendrites** are long, thin branches that grow from the cell body. They extend outward and branch again and again, becoming thinner each time, like a tree's branches and twigs. They receive nerve messages from other nerve cells and convey them toward the nerve cell body.
- The **axon**, or nerve fiber, is a long, wire-like extension of the nerve cell body. It may have its own finger-like branches, the fiber terminal. The main task of this fiber is to carry nerve signals away from the nerve cell body and to pass them to other nerve cells.

Nerve cell types

The structure of nerve cells in the brain varies. Some have very short or branching fibers. Some have just a few dendrites, while others have thousands. Some have a cell body halfway along the fiber, rather than near one end.

Also, some nerve cell fibers are myelinated. This means they have a covering, or sheath, wrapped around them, made of the fatty substance **myelin**. The sheath protects the fiber and stops its messages from leaking away. It also allows messages to travel fast, at 100 meters (328 feet) per second or more. Other fibers are un-myelinated and carry nerve messages more slowly, at a speed of 1 to 2 meters (3 to 6 feet) per second.

Nerve signals

A single nerve signal is a tiny, brief pulse of electricity. It is created by the movement of dissolved **mineral** substances, called **ions**. Ions have electrical charges and are either positive or negative. They include sodium (Na+) and potassium (K+) ions.

Nerve signals do not pass inside the nerve cell, but rather along its outer layer, called the nerve cell membrane. This has tiny structures in it called ion pumps and channels. They are specialized to pass certain ions through the membrane, which normally acts as a barrier to them.

The nerve impulse

A "resting" part of the nerve cell membrane, when no signal is passing, has more sodium ions outside, in the fluid around the cell, and more potassium ions inside the cell. As a nerve signal arrives, sodium pumps in the membrane pass sodium ions from outside to inside. Then potassium pumps do the same, but in the reverse direction, inside to outside. These rapid movements of ions cause a "spike" of electricity, known as the action potential, nerve impulse, or wave of depolarization. This is the nerve signal.

This microscopic view of the brain shows two nerve cell bodies (green blobs). Dendrites extend from them into the complicated network of dendrites from other nerve cells.

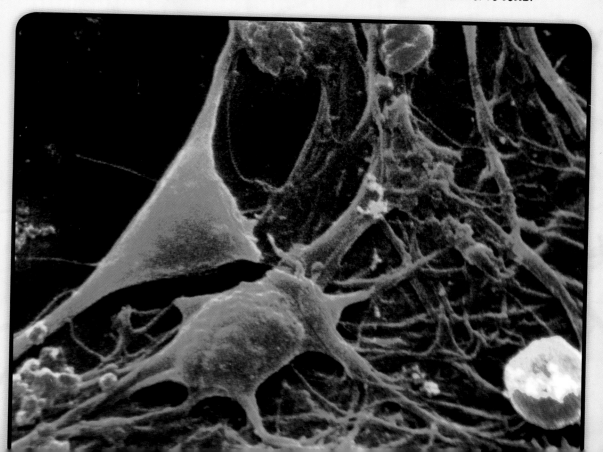

15

Signals Around the Brain

As we move around, see, listen, speak, and think, millions of nerve signals come into the brain, pass around its various parts, and pass out again. The signals travel very fast, at a rate of many feet every second, through trillions of individual nerve cells.

Yet nerve cells do not actually touch one another. Where their dendrites and fibers come together, they are separated by tiny gaps, called **synapses**. Nerve signals pass across these gaps by batches of specialized body chemicals, known as **neurotransmitters**.

A gap in the way

At the nerve junction, or synapse, the membranes of two nerve cells are separated by a gap, called the synaptic cleft. As an electrical nerve impulse reaches the synapse, it causes the release of tiny amounts of chemicals, known as neurotransmitters. These flow across the gap and "land on" the membrane of the receiving nerve cell, where they fit into specialized sites, called **receptors**. They alter the membrane in such a way that the original wave of electricity from the sending nerve cell begins again in the receiving nerve cell.

Yes and no

A single nerve signal "jumps" from one nerve cell to the next, as described above. However, the nervous system is much more complicated. Sometimes the receiving nerve cell does not "fire" its own nerve signal until it has received several nerve impulses in quick succession from sending nerve cells.

Also, while some nerve signals from a sending nerve cell cause impulses in a receiving nerve cell, others "damp down" the response of the receiving nerve cell, so no signals are sent. In addition, many nerve cells have not just a few synapses, but rather thousands, and are linked to many different nerve cells.

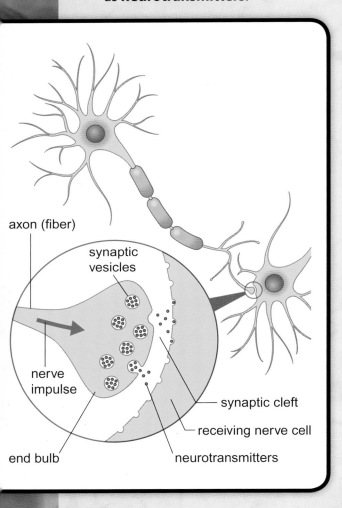

axon (fiber)

synaptic vesicles

nerve impulse

synaptic cleft

receiving nerve cell

end bulb

neurotransmitters

A tiny gap, the synaptic cleft, separates two nerve cells at a synapse. The circle shows an enlarged view, with neurotransmitter chemicals passing across the gap.

The timing of nerve signals, such as how many there are in a burst, also affects how they are received and sent on. The nerve cells also form new synapses with other nerve cells, and they lose old synapses. This is like a computer continually "rewiring" itself, according to its experiences and what has happened. Nerve cells create new pathways, or circuits, for nerve signals around the system.

Patterns of signals

The overall result is that the possible pathways for nerve messages around the brain are endless. They also change every day, week, month, and year. This is a central feature of the brain, as shown on later pages. Our awareness, thoughts, decisions, feelings, intentions, ideas, learning, and memories are all patterns of nerve signals passing around the nerve cells of the brain, and they change constantly.

People talk to different individuals at different times. Nerve cells are similar, passing information by numerous and changing links, called synapses.

IN FOCUS: JUMPING ACROSS THE SYNAPSE GAP

The tiny gap in the junction, or synapse, between two nerve cells is about one-hundredth of the width of a human hair. The time taken for neurotransmitter chemicals to pass across it is about one-thousandth of a second.

Brain Stem

The brain stem is partly a highway for nerve fibers carrying messages between other parts of the brain and the spinal cord. It is also the body's "automatic pilot." It houses many control centers for body activities that usually happen in an automatic or reflexive way, when we do not have to think about them. These centers are part of the reticular formation. This is a series of long, slim bundles of nerve cells with their nerve fibers, lying in the center of the brain stem.

The brain stem has three main parts: the **medulla** oblongata, pons, and midbrain.

Medulla oblongata

The "stalk" for the whole brain is called the medulla oblongata. It tapers into the spinal cord beneath. It is about 3 centimeters (1 inch) tall and wide, and it contains several important control centers:

- The cardiac center regulates the heartbeat.
- The respiratory center controls breathing.
- The vasomotor center regulates the width of blood vessels and affects blood pressure.
- The medulla oblongata also contains control centers for sneezing, coughing, swallowing, and vomiting.

Pons

The egg-shaped pons, or "bridge," is chiefly a throughway, or "bypass," for nerve signals. It also contains two centers that work with the respiratory center in the medulla oblongata to control breathing.

Midbrain

The midbrain is not actually in the middle of the whole brain, but just below. Like the pons, it contains control centers. Some of these coordinate the way the eyes focus, to see clearly, and also how they move or swivel in their sockets, as the head turns to watch a fast-moving object, such as a racing car. Other control centers pass nerve messages from the ears, about hearing, to the upper parts of the brain.

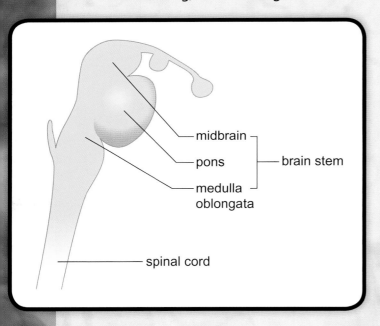

midbrain
pons — brain stem
medulla oblongata

spinal cord

The brain stem consists of several parts in the lowest regions of the brain. (The upper and rear parts, the cerebrum and cerebellum, are not shown here.)

 Aircraft can run on autopilot. The brain stem has a similar function, but relies on the quick-thinking upper brain for fast action and split-second decisions.

On either side of the uppermost midbrain is a rounded, dark-colored part, called the substantia nigra. This is involved in the condition known as Parkinson's disease (see page 35).

Crossover—when left is right

Many nerve fibers pass through the brain stem, linking body parts and the spinal cord to the upper parts of the brain. In the medulla oblongata, these bundles cross over from one side to the other, forming an X shape.

The crossover structure means that the left side of the brain receives signals from, and sends signals to, the right side of the body, and vice versa. So, each side of the brain deals with sensations from, and controls the muscles in, the opposite side of the body.

HEALTH FOCUS: Brain stem death

The brain stem is essential for life. It contains centers that control important processes, such as breathing and heartbeat. For this reason, doctors check this part of the brain when a person has suffered a severe head injury or a very serious illness. Sometimes a stopped heart, or still lungs, can be started again by emergency medical treatment. If the brain stem is not active, however, there is almost no hope of recovery. This is called brain stem inactivity, or "brain death."

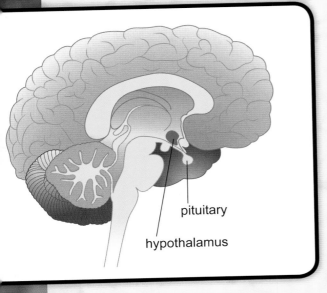

pituitary

hypothalamus

The hypothalamus is at the lower front of the brain, roughly midway between both eyes and both ears. It is small, forming less than one two-hundredth of the brain's total size. It contains many important control centers for essential body processes and affects many kinds of behavior, including moods and emotions, and basic desires such as thirst, hunger, sexual behavior, and sleep patterns.

Monitoring the body

The hypothalamus contains specialized **sensory** cells that monitor conditions inside the body. These conditions include levels of substances in the blood, such as water and glucose, and blood temperature.

The hypothalamus is about the size of a grape. Yet it is a major monitoring and control center in the brain.

If conditions vary from normal, the hypothalamus sends out nerve messages to other parts of the brain and also directly to body parts, in order to bring the conditions back to normal again. This is part of the overall body process known as **homeostasis**. Homeostasis keeps internal conditions fairly constant, within a narrow range, so that all body parts can work effectively.

Homeostasis

As an example of homeostasis, the hypothalamus contains thirst centers that check the amount of water in the blood. If this falls, the centers make us aware that we need to take in extra fluids by drinking. The centers also save water in the body by making the kidneys lose less water in urine. Similarly, hunger centers in the hypothalamus control our desire to eat.

Links with the ANS

The hypothalamus uses two other body systems as its "servants." One is the autonomic nervous system (ANS). It carries nerve messages from the hypothalamus to the heart, lungs, digestive system, kidneys, skin, and many other parts. These activities are **involuntary**, which means we do not have to think about them. They automatically keep the body running smoothly.

Links with the hormonal system

A stalk from the hypothalamus connects it to a small **hormonal gland**, called the **pituitary**, situated below. The pituitary is the major gland of the whole hormonal (endocrine) system. It controls many glands around the body and is controlled by the hypothalamus. In this way, the two systems, nervous and hormonal, work closely together to regulate body functions.

Too cold

Temperature sensors in the hypothalamus control body temperature. If it falls below a certain level, the hypothalamus sends out nerve messages to blood vessels near the skin, making them narrower, so less heat is lost from the warm blood through the skin. It also tells sweat glands to release less sweat, muscles to twitch ("shiver"), and body cells to work faster and to burn more high-energy sugars. All these processes help to make the body warmer. If the body gets too hot, the reverse happens (see box). In this way, body temperature is kept within a very narrow range, usually less than 1°C (1.8°F).

Have you ever felt the urge to cool down by eating ice cream? This is the result of the hypothalamus at work. It monitors rising body temperature by amounts smaller than one-hundredth of 1°C (1.8°F). It begins automatic cooling processes and also makes the thinking brain alter our behavior in order to bring down the temperature.

HEALTH FOCUS: When the body "overheats"

In some conditions, such as playing active sports on a warm day, the body gets too hot. The hypothalamus detects this and reverses the warming process (described at left). It is important to take a break and to allow the body to cool itself naturally in this way. Cool water sprays can help, as can staying in the shade and exposing the skin to a fan or to the breeze.

Emotions and the Body Clock

The hypothalamus is not only the chief controller of automatic body processes. It is also involved in the types of behavior we show during strong emotions and moods.

Danger!

Do you remember how you felt the last time you faced danger or worry? Your body reacted with signs of fearful behavior. These usually include a faster heartbeat and breathing, tensed muscles, dry mouth, sweaty skin, eyes wide open, fluttery feelings of "butterflies" inside, and, for some people, crying and shouting and waving their arms in panic.

From thoughts to actions

These reactions are brought about by the hypothalamus, using its links with the autonomic nervous and hormonal systems. They prepare the body for fast response and physical action. The hypothalamus only starts these reactions after it receives messages from the "thinking" part of the brain, the cortex. Once the reactions begin, it is very difficult to stop them by conscious thought. They are carried out through the autonomic nervous system, and they progress automatically.

Similar reactions occur with other powerful emotions, such as anger, rage, pain, and great pleasure. They are controlled by the hypothalamus, but in response to instructions from the cortex.

Being able to control your emotions is an important skill. Professional athletes often undergo training to learn how to do just that. However, once great panic or rage begins, it is difficult to control. The body's automatic nervous and hormonal processes take over from the conscious, thinking mind for a time.

The body clock

The hypothalamus contains the "body clock"—a small group of nerve cells, called the supra-chiasmatic nucleus (SCN). It is so named because it is just above the optic chiasma, a crossover junction (chiasma) of nerves carrying signals from the eyes to the brain.

SCN cells have a natural, built-in cycle of activity of about 24 hours. They send nerve signals to many parts of the brain, to control a vast array of **biorhythms**—body processes that vary in a regular way, day and night. These include body temperature, hormone levels, urine formation, digestive activity, injury repair, alertness, and, of course, waking and sleeping.

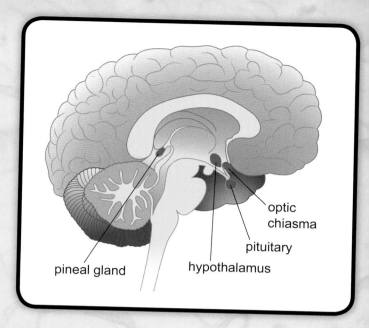

The SCN is in the lower front of the hypothalamus, just above the crossover of nerves from the eyes, the optic chiasma.

Adjusting the clock

The SCN receives signals from the optic nerves just below it, bringing information from the eyes about levels of daylight and darkness. The signals continually adjust the clock so that it runs to an accurate 24-hour rhythm. In this way, the body's natural rhythms of alertness, rest, waking, and sleeping stay in step with the days and nights of the outside world.

Tests on people who stay in constant daylight or darkness show that the SCN still works. The people wake up, eat, are active, rest, and sleep in the usual daily cycle. Without changing light levels to adjust the "body clock," it tends to run slightly slower, with a cycle of about 25 hours.

IN FOCUS: PINEAL GLAND

The pineal gland, or pineal body, just above the thalamus, has close links with the hypothalamus, and especially with the SCN. It carries out a similar role to that of the hypothalamus, and it links brain activity to the hormonal system. In particular, it makes and releases the sleep hormone, melatonin, under instructions from the SCN.

Sleeping Brain

The brain's hypothalamus, SCN, and pineal gland control many natural rhythms, or daily cycles, of activity in the body. Perhaps the most obvious biorhythm is the wake-sleep cycle. As we go to sleep, our muscles relax and our heartbeat and breathing slow. The brain, however, stays very busy, as shown by recordings of brain waves, using an electroencephalograph (**EEG**) machine.

As we fall asleep, brain waves become longer and lower. This is called slow-wave, orthodox, or deep sleep. It is difficult to wake the person. Sometimes we say he or she is "dead to the world"!

REM sleep and dreams

After 50 to 70 minutes of deep sleep, the brain waves become faster, taller, and more irregular. Also, breathing and heart rate quicken and muscles twitch. The eyes flick rapidly back and forth under closed lids. This stage is **REM** (rapid eye movement) **sleep**, also called paradoxical or shallow sleep.

After 15 to 30 minutes of REM sleep, the brain sinks into deeper sleep again. These periods of deep sleep and REM sleep alternate every 90 to 100 minutes. After a total sleep time of about seven to eight hours, the average adult wakes.

People woken during REM sleep usually report that they have been dreaming. In fact, most of us probably dream each night during REM sleep. Only if we wake up during, or just after, the REM period do we actually recall the dreams.

 The sleeping body seems still and inactive. But essential actions, such as breathing and heartbeat, still happen under the control of the brain, which is also very busy with other processes. However, much of what the brain does during sleep remains a mystery.

Why do we sleep and dream?

There have been many ideas about why we sleep and dream. One is that, since we are sight-based beings and cannot see to move around in the dark, we sleep to avoid danger, as the body rests and repairs itself. Another idea is that dreams could be the random activity of nerve cells in the brain, with little meaning. Alternatively, dreams are when the brain sorts out its recent thoughts and memories, and throws out information that is not important. Dreams could even be "mini dramas," when the brain works through emotional problems and conflicts.

Several kinds of research have shown that sleep and dreams are important in forming memories. People with disturbed sleep find it more difficult to remember, and especially to recall recent events in their "working memory." Sleep also helps to form long-term memories.

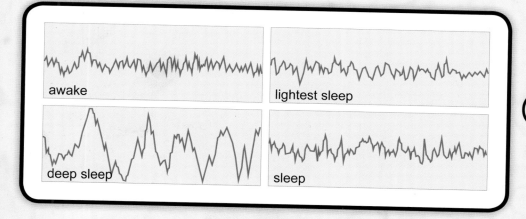

awake

lightest sleep

deep sleep

sleep

Recordings by an EEG machine show many different types of electrical activity in the brain during sleep.

HEALTH FOCUS: Sleeping pills

Various medicinal drugs work as sleeping pills, to reduce brain activity and to bring on feelings of tiredness and sleep. Most work by interfering with neurotransmitters, such as serotonin, acetylcholine, **adrenaline** (epinephrine), and nor-adrenaline (nor-epinephrine). However, some of these drugs can cause dependency and other problems.

Cerebellum and Movement

You do not have to concentrate in great detail on every tiny action you make. You decide to write your name or tie your shoelaces or ride your bicycle—and then you find yourself doing so, almost "without thinking." Making complicated, skilled movements involves part of the brain called the cerebellum.

The cerebellum is tucked under the rear of the cerebrum and has a similar wrinkled, folded appearance. It makes up about one-tenth of the total brain volume. It has millions of nerve connections, especially with the large domed cerebrum above, and the medulla and spinal cord to the front and below.

Posture and balance

We can stand up straight, walk, lean, bend, and jog with almost no conscious thought. Parts in the middle and base of the cerebellum control these actions. They respond to information coming into the brain from the ears (including the balance sensors), the eyes, and the stretch sensors in muscles and joints. Together, these messages tell the brain about the position and movements of various body parts, especially the head, neck, and trunk.

The cerebellum sorts through the messages and sends out instructions to muscles, again mainly in the head, neck, and trunk. The muscles work in a precise way to keep the body moving smoothly in a well-balanced manner, so we do not stumble or fall.

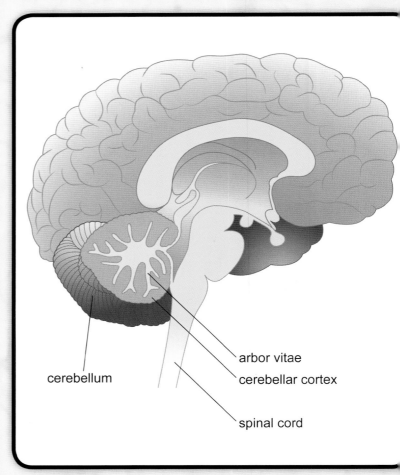

cerebellum

arbor vitae

cerebellar cortex

spinal cord

The cerebellum is the rear-lowermost part of the brain, at the back of the brain stem. It has a complicated branching pattern inside, called the arbor vitae, or "living tree."

 A skilled skier tries tiny adjustments to achieve an even faster trip down the slope. The main body movements for speed and balance are carried out, almost in an automatic way, by the cerebellum.

Skilled movements

Two parts of the cerebellum, called lateral **lobes**, one on each side, help to control skilled, precise movements of the arms, hands, legs, and feet. These actions do not start here, however. The decision to move a body part comes from a higher part of the brain, called the **motor** cortex. When it arrives as nerve messages at the cerebellum, the cerebellum "fills in the details." It sends out thousands of precise complex nerve messages to dozens of muscles, so they pull with exactly the right strength and timing, to make the whole movement smooth and coordinated.

The cerebellum also checks movements as they happen and fine-tunes them with small adjustments. Only if a drastic problem occurs does the cerebellum send signals back to the cortex, so that our thoughts turn to dealing with the problem.

IN FOCUS:
"LITTLE BRAIN"

"Cerebellum" means "little brain," and the cerebellum looks like a smaller version of the whole brain. It has two domed hemispheres, each with a wrinkled gray surface, called the cortex, containing mainly nerve cell bodies and dendrites. Beneath are white masses of nerve fibers leading to other parts of the brain.

The Brain's Nerves

Often, a computer is "hot-wired" directly to its most important devices, such as the mouse, keyboard, and screen. It does not receive or send signals to these parts through a general network. The **cranial** nerves are like the brain's "hot-wires." They branch directly from the brain as 12 pairs. There is a left and right nerve in each pair, linking the brain directly to body parts, mostly in the head.

Cranial nerves are known both by their names and numbers, 1–12 (or Roman numerals I–XII). Pairs 1 and 2 join to the cerebrum. The others join to the brain stem. Some cranial nerves are sensory, carrying information to the brain. Others are motor, conveying nerve messages away from the brain, to muscles and glands. Some are both sensory and motor and are known as mixed nerves.

Brain and body

Cranial nerve 10 (vagus) is the largest of the cranial nerves and has the most connections. It branches down to the heart, lungs, stomach, intestines, liver, and kidneys. Various parts of the brain, especially the hypothalamus and medulla oblongata, receive and send signals along this nerve. It is part of the autonomic, or automatic, monitoring and control of body processes.

 Speaking involves several cranial nerves, especially 11 and 12 (see chart opposite), which control the larynx (voice box) and tongue.

HEALTH FOCUS: Facial palsy

"Palsy" is muscle weakness, or paralysis. Facial palsy (Bell's palsy) affects cranial nerve 7 (facial), which becomes swollen and pinched where it passes through and along the skull bone. The cause is not clear, although the problem can be set off by a cold wind on the face. The effects are weakness and drooping of one side of the face, with the inability to close the eye, smile, or make facial expressions. Taste may also be affected. The condition usually clears up in a few weeks, perhaps aided by medication.

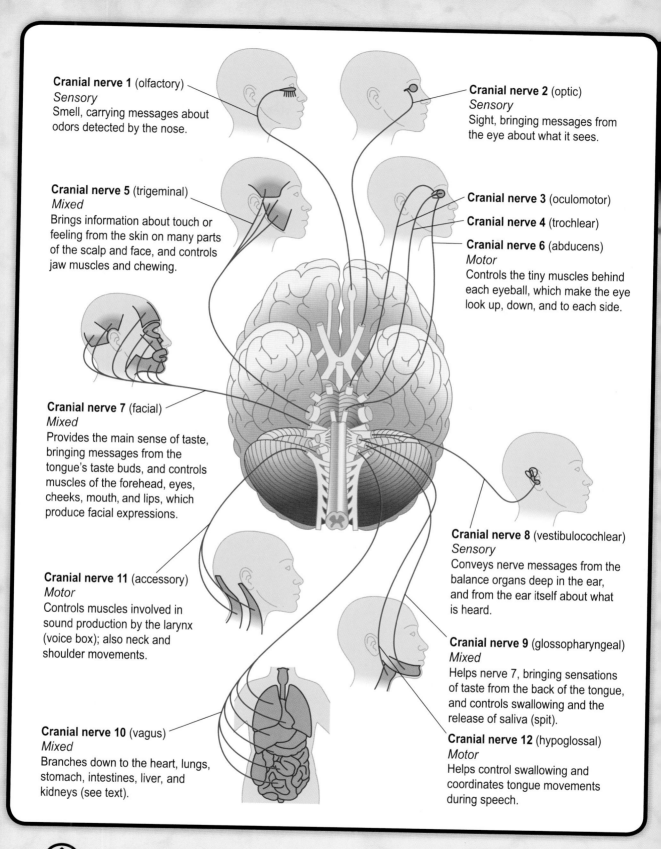

Cranial nerve 1 (olfactory)
Sensory
Smell, carrying messages about odors detected by the nose.

Cranial nerve 2 (optic)
Sensory
Sight, bringing messages from the eye about what it sees.

Cranial nerve 5 (trigeminal)
Mixed
Brings information about touch or feeling from the skin on many parts of the scalp and face, and controls jaw muscles and chewing.

Cranial nerve 3 (oculomotor)
Cranial nerve 4 (trochlear)
Cranial nerve 6 (abducens)
Motor
Controls the tiny muscles behind each eyeball, which make the eye look up, down, and to each side.

Cranial nerve 7 (facial)
Mixed
Provides the main sense of taste, bringing messages from the tongue's taste buds, and controls muscles of the forehead, eyes, cheeks, mouth, and lips, which produce facial expressions.

Cranial nerve 8 (vestibulocochlear)
Sensory
Conveys nerve messages from the balance organs deep in the ear, and from the ear itself about what is heard.

Cranial nerve 11 (accessory)
Motor
Controls muscles involved in sound production by the larynx (voice box); also neck and shoulder movements.

Cranial nerve 9 (glossopharyngeal)
Mixed
Helps nerve 7, bringing sensations of taste from the back of the tongue, and controls swallowing and the release of saliva (spit).

Cranial nerve 10 (vagus)
Mixed
Branches down to the heart, lungs, stomach, intestines, liver, and kidneys (see text).

Cranial nerve 12 (hypoglossal)
Motor
Helps control swallowing and coordinates tongue movements during speech.

The 12 pairs of cranial nerves branch directly from the brain's underside, mainly out to parts of the face, head, and neck. Cranial nerve 10 runs down through the neck to parts in the chest and lower body.

Cerebral Cortex

The outer layer of the brain's main part, the cerebrum, is called the cerebral cortex. It is about 3 millimeters (0.12 inches) thick, gray in color, and folded into bulges and grooves, which increase its surface area to about the size of a pillowcase. The cortex contains more than 50 billion nerve cells, with their cell bodies, spider-like dendrites, and nerve fibers passing to the inner brain parts.

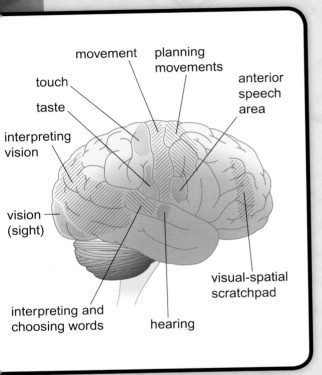

movement
planning movements
touch
anterior speech area
taste
interpreting vision
vision (sight)
visual-spatial scratchpad
interpreting and choosing words
hearing

Areas of the cortex, the outer layer of the cerebrum, deal with different parts of the body and various parts of our thinking or mental processes.

Centers of the cortex

The cortex is the "thinking brain." It is the main site for conscious thoughts, where we are aware of our surroundings, our actions, and ourselves. On each side, it is divided into larger bulges called lobes. In each of these lobes, different parts called areas, or centers, deal with nerve messages coming in or going out to certain body parts.

Frontal lobe

The frontal lobe is under the forehead. The front part of it, sometimes known as the prefrontal lobe, is involved with expressing excitement and emotional feelings.

On the side of the frontal lobe is an area involved in "working memory." This is not so much a storage site for the short-term memories themselves, but rather an organizing area that tells other parts of the brain to store memories and then recalls them when needed. This area also helps us to create a picture memory of our immediate surroundings so that we can move around without bumping into things.

Toward the rear of the frontal lobe is a strip down the side, called the motor cortex. It oversees muscle control to make bodily movements. At the rear lower corner is the Broca's, or anterior, speech area, which is involved in speech.

Parietal lobe

The parietal lobe is at the rear of the brain. At its front is a strip down the side, called the touch cortex. It receives information from the skin about what we touch and feel. Like the motor cortex just in front, different patches of the touch cortex deal with different body parts—face, head, neck, torso, arm, and so on. The lowest part of this area deals with taste information. The parietal lobe, like the frontal lobe, also has areas involved in "working memory."

 When we look at a screen intently, the lower rear part of the cortex, known as the visual center, is very active, interpreting what the eyes see.

Temporal lobe

The temporal lobe is under the temple (above the ear). It contains the **auditory** cortex, which sorts information from the ear about what we hear. It also contains the vestibular cortex, which maintains balance and posture, and part of the Wernicke's, or posterior, speech area.

Occipital lobe

The occipital lobe, at the lower rear of the brain, is mostly concerned with receiving and sorting nerve messages from the eyes. The visual cortex has several centers that deal with different aspects of vision, such as what the eye sees in various parts of a scene, recognizing items from memory, identifying them, and putting the parts together into a meaningful overall picture. The lobe also contains part of the Wernicke's speech area.

HEALTH FOCUS: Forced time out

In many sports, any head injury that is followed by a blackout, or concussion, means that the player must leave the action and have an urgent medical check. This is often followed by rest for days or possibly weeks. If the brain parts controlling movements are not working well, athletes are more likely to put themselves in danger with clumsy, awkward movements or slow reactions.

Two Sides of the Brain

The main part of the brain, the cerebrum, is made of two halves, known as the cerebral hemispheres. As explained earlier, nerve fibers from one side of the body cross to the other side in the lower brain. The left cerebral hemisphere deals with nerve signals from and to the right side of the body, and the right hemisphere deals with signals to and from the left side of the body.

A strap-like "bridge" of more than 200 million nerve fibers, called the corpus callosum, links the two hemispheres. This allows them to share information and send signals to each other.

One side takes over

The cerebral hemispheres look similar. In a very young child, they also work in a similar way. Gradually, by the age of five to eight years, one side becomes dominant (in control). This is usually the left hemisphere, which controls the right side of the body, including the right hand. Most people (about nine out of ten) use mainly their right hand for precise, intricate tasks. Even in most left-handed people, the left hemisphere is dominant.

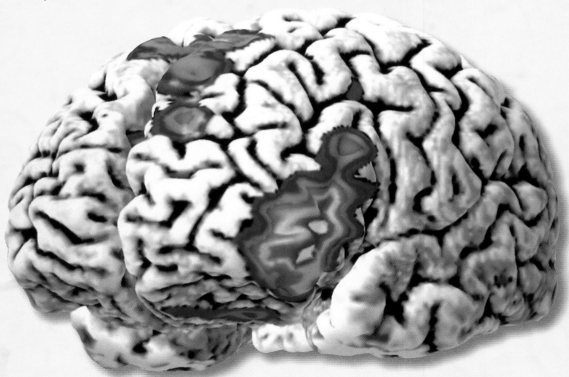

The left side of the brain usually dominates the right side and controls the right side of the body. So, detailed hand movements for a right-handed person, and the main control of speech, come from the left cerebral hemisphere. The areas colored above are associated with speech.

HEALTH FOCUS: Dyslexia

Dyslexia is a group of conditions that affect a child's ability to read, write, spell, and learn. In many cases, the child is otherwise normal, or has above-average mental skills. Aspects of dyslexia include reading letters or words backward, such as "b" instead of "d," or "on" for "no."

Different forms of dyslexia have different causes. These include **genetic** influences (inherited from parents), the way nerves develop in the unborn baby's brain, and the way the eyes and brain work together. Some children with dyslexia have learning difficulties, simply for the reason that they cannot read properly. If their dyslexia is identified early, and followed by expert therapy, they can learn to read well and progress at the same rate as their peers. Treatment of these conditions is increasingly successful.

Speech

Most processes in the brain happen by connections between several parts. Speech is an example. The left (dominant) posterior speech area recognizes and understands spoken words and selects the words for a reply. The left anterior speech area then organizes the patterns of nerve messages to speak the reply.

Two halves make the whole

There are general differences in the way that the two hemispheres of the brain work. The left side is more concerned with language, reason, logic, numbers, math, figuring out steps and stages, and how individual pieces function. It is the "parts" side of the brain.

The right hemisphere is the "whole" side. It deals more with general ideas and concepts, overall shapes, colors and forms (such as quickly recognizing a face), art and music awareness, intuition, and "jumping" to an idea or conclusion.

The left side of the brain tends to pick out details, while the right side sees and understands the whole idea. Both sides work together and help each other.

The right side of the brain usually takes charge in creative and artistic activities, such as painting a mural.

At the Center of the Brain

Under the "thinking" part of the brain, the cortex, are bundles of nerve fibers called **white matter**. They carry messages between the cortex and many other brain parts. One part is the thalamus, which monitors sensory information (except for smell) coming from other brain parts toward the cortex, and checks whether it is important. For example, as you sleep, your ears hear normal nighttime sounds. If there is a strange sound, the thalamus identifies it, and you wake up. The thalamus is also involved in control of movements, biorhythms, and our level of alertness, from fully alert to resting, drowsy, or asleep.

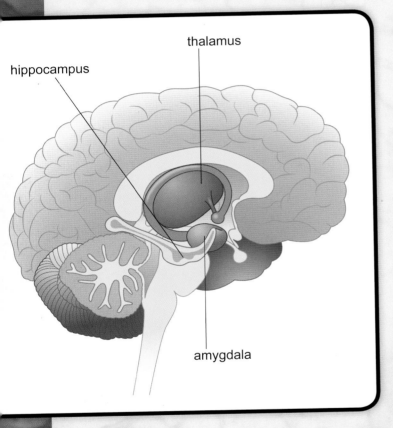

hippocampus

thalamus

amygdala

The middle parts of the brain are involved in a wide variety of mental processes, including conscious thought, precise movements, and forming memories.

Basal ganglia and limbic system

In the lower center of each cerebral hemisphere are groups of **gray matter**, called basal **ganglia**. They have many links with the cortex and the thalamus. They are involved with movements and behavior, especially in making actions smooth and purposeful.

The limbic lobe is a ring-shaped region on the lower, inward-facing surface of each cerebral hemisphere. It works with other parts of the brain as the limbic system. This takes part in memory and emotions, as well as the reactions and behavior they cause. For example, when we recall a frightening event from long ago, which still makes us feel cold and clammy, with a racing heart, this is due partly to the limbic system.

A patch on the limbic lobe surface is called the olfactory cortex, or "smell center." It deals with nerve messages coming from the nose. Such close links with the limbic system mean that certain smells can cause powerful memories and feelings.

HEALTH FOCUS:
Parkinson's disease

Parkinson's disease mainly affects the parts of the brain called the basal ganglia. It is caused by problems with chemicals called neurotransmitters. The brain cannot control movements normally, especially actions we do almost without thinking, such as swinging the arms when walking. The disease causes shaking or trembling, slow or jerky movements, muscle stiffness, and changed posture. A person with the condition tends to walk with a stoop, using short, shuffling steps.

After the age of 60, about 1 person in 200 develops Parkinson's disease. The misuse of drugs and certain brain infections can produce similar symptoms, called Parkinsonism. Several kinds of medications and other treatments, such as modern forms of surgery, and perhaps the future use of **stem cells** or gene therapy, may be very helpful to lessen the symptoms and slow the progress of the condition.

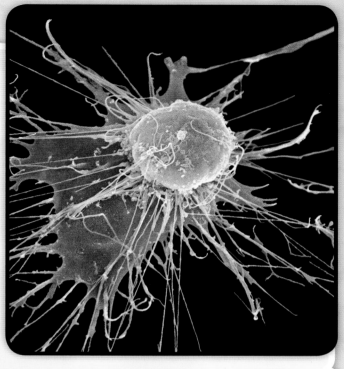

Stem cells have the ability to develop into various kinds of specialized cells, including nerve cells. They are being tested in several brain conditions.

IN FOCUS: MEMORY

There is no single "memory center" in the brain. Many parts are involved, including the cortex (especially of the frontal lobe), hippocampus, amygdala, and thalamus. The information of memories is probably stored as pathways among the trillions of interconnected nerve cells.

Short-term or working memory is when we retain facts for seconds or minutes, such as a telephone number you are about to call. By the next day, the memory has gone. The hippocampus helps to convert short-term memories to long-term ones. This is particularly useful for important information that we need for weeks, years, or a lifetime, such as our names and where we live.

Brain Infections

Certain germs (harmful **microbes**) can infect the brain, either as their main site of attack, or as part of an infection elsewhere in the body. Infection in the brain itself is quite rare. Many germs travel around the body and reach the brain in the blood. However, the blood vessels in the brain have a special structure in their walls, which limits what can pass through. This is called the "blood-brain barrier." Unfortunately, the same barrier also limits the ability of medicinal drugs to pass from the blood into the brain itself.

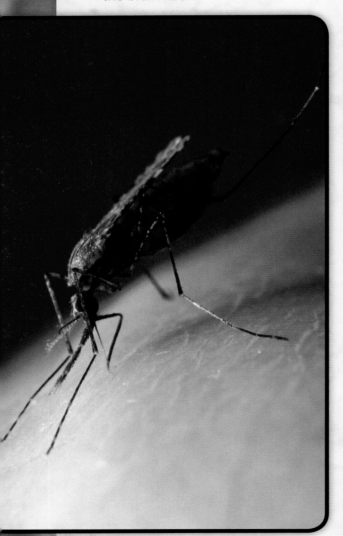

Some germs are types of **bacteria**, which can generally be attacked with **antibiotic** drugs. Other germs include **viruses**, which are rarely affected by antibiotics, but can be treated by a growing range of antiviral drugs.

Encephalitis

Swelling and **inflammation** of the brain itself is known as encephalitis. It may be caused by a virus, either as the main site of infection, or as part of another viral disease, such as mumps or measles.

Mosquitoes and ticks spread some kinds of encephalitis virus. In tropical regions, tiny single-celled parasites can cause the problem—for example, the sleeping sickness parasite spread by tsetse flies.

Symptoms of encephalitis may be similar to those of any mild illness, such as a headache, raised temperature, and feeling tired. The symptoms may progress to more serious drowsiness, fear of bright light, loss of muscle power, disturbed speech and sight, and even unconsciousness.

With good care and medication, most people recover from encephalitis. However, there is a risk of brain damage or even death for babies, older people, and those with other illnesses.

 Mosquitoes, such as the one shown here, infect people with cerebral malaria as they take blood.

Meningitis

In a healthy person, the cerebrospinal fluid around the brain is clear and watery. In some infections, it becomes milky or cloudy. This occurs especially in meningitis, which is swelling, or inflammation, of the layers around the brain, called the meninges.

The germs may spread from an infection elsewhere, such as the ear, or be part of a general infection, such as tuberculosis or mumps. In some cases, the germs enter through a head wound or injury. Certain viruses that cause meningitis spread through the air, affecting a number of people in the same area and causing a small **epidemic**.

Other brain infections

In some cases of the tropical disease malaria, the brain is severely affected. This is known as cerebral malaria, and it may cause symptoms similar to those of a stroke, perhaps with seizures. It requires urgent medical attention.

The condition of AIDS, caused by HIV (human immunodeficiency virus), may affect the brain and cause various symptoms.

HEALTH FOCUS: Effects of meningitis

There are many forms of meningitis, both viral and bacterial, and they vary from mild to life-threatening. Symptoms include a headache, fever, stiff neck, nausea, vomiting, and fear of bright light. There may also be a dark skin rash. Without urgent medical treatment, some sufferers become drowsy and lose consciousness.

The condition is often more dangerous in babies and young children. They cannot describe their symptoms well, and they are at greater risk of brain damage and permanent disability.

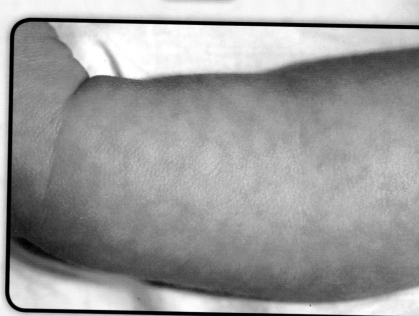

A red or dark skin rash, looking as though the person is hot and flushed, is one possible symptom of meningitis. Unlike other rashes, the dark color may not get lighter if the area is pressed.

Brain Disorders

The brain can feel pain in all parts of the body—except itself. It does not have suitable pain-sensing nerves. A headache is not usually a "brain-ache," but rather pain from the blood vessels, nerves, or meninges around the brain. A headache is usually a symptom of another problem, not a disorder itself. Causes of headaches vary hugely, from a head injury or food allergy to a bodily infection, a brain **tumor**, a period of physical or emotional **stress**, or the effects of drugs, such as alcohol.

Migraine

Severe headaches that tend to come back, often on one side of the head, are known as migraines. There are usually other symptoms before or with the headache, such as nausea or vomiting, disturbed vision, or being sensitive to noises. Sometimes, before the migraine, there is a strange feeling or sensation, such as flashing lights or zigzag lines in front of the eyes.

Some migraines are brought on by "triggers," which vary from emotional stress or high blood pressure to eating chocolate or drinking alcohol. Cases of migraines can also run in families. In many instances, the pain seems to be due to narrowing, then widening, of the blood vessels in or around the brain. Modern medicinal drugs are very effective at helping most migraine sufferers.

 This girl is undergoing an electroencephalograph (EEG) examination (see box on page 39). The electrode sensors on her head pick up tiny electrical signals of brain activity. These are then mapped and shown on the screen. This process is known as Brain Electrical Activity Mapping (BEAM).

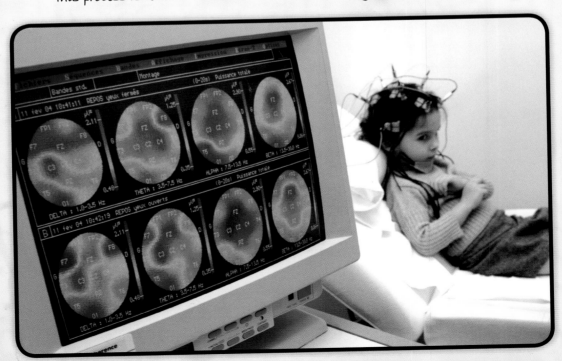

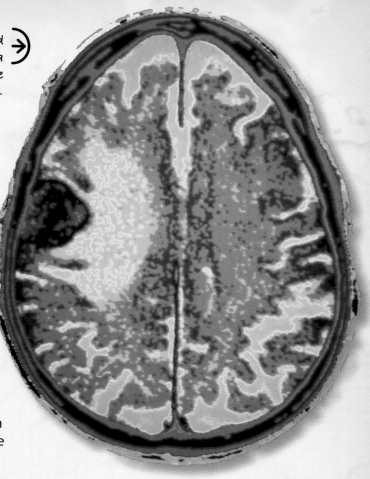

This colored computed tomography (CT) scan shows a human brain with brain cancer (the dark blue patch on the left).

Seizures and epilepsy

There are many forms of seizure. They vary in intensity from a brief period of faintness, perhaps with strange sensations such as an odd taste in the mouth, to a severe attack, with a blackout and violent, uncontrolled movements called **convulsions**. These types of events are often known as epilepsy, although this is a term used to describe a wide variety of conditions.

Some kinds of epilepsy have a known cause, such as a brain tumor. In other cases, nerve cells seem to fire at random as a kind of "electrical storm" rages in the brain. Between 1 person in 100 and 1 in 200 develops epilepsy, although this varies in different regions around the world. Drugs called anticonvulsants are successful at treating most cases.

Brain tumors

A tumor can occur in the brain, often for no clear reason. It tends to press on the brain and cause various symptoms, depending on its location. These vary from headaches and nausea or vomiting, to sight problems, loss of balance or sense of smell, seizures, muscle weakness, and even a changed personality. Treatment may include an operation, **radiotherapy** (radiation treatment), medicinal drugs, or all three. Generally, the sooner treatment begins, the higher its success rate.

IN FOCUS:
BRAIN WAVES

Millions of electrical nerve signals pass around the brain every second. Sensor pads placed on the skin of the head can detect these signals. They show up as wavy lines on the screen or paper strip of an EEG machine. The size and shape of the brain waves help scientists to study what the normal brain does— for example, when asleep. EEG recordings are also very helpful to doctors when identifying disorders, such as epilepsy and stroke.

Brain Development

The brain is one of the first body parts to develop. About three weeks after life begins in the womb, the whole body is slightly smaller than a grain of rice and shaped like a letter C. At this stage, there is no sign of a head end with a brain inside. From the fourth week, the brain grows faster than any other body part. It bulges hugely, becoming almost one-third of the size of the whole tiny body, with the spinal cord as its "tail." Nerves begin to grow and branch from it, as the eyes and other parts of the face and head take shape.

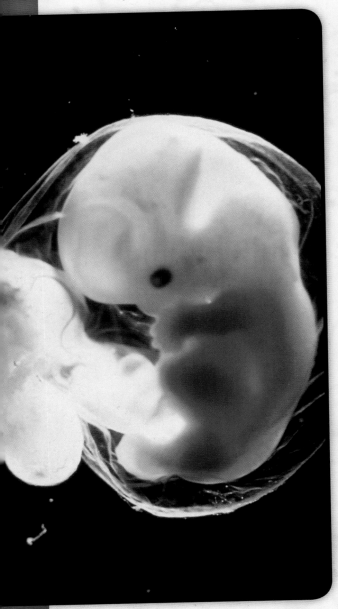

After this early burst of brain growth, other body parts begin to catch up as the baby develops in the womb. By about week 12, the overall shape of the brain is formed, but the cerebral hemispheres are still smooth. Their first wrinkles or grooves appear over the next few weeks.

Invisible growth

A new baby's brain weighs about 350 grams (12.3 ounces), slightly less than one-quarter of its adult size. This is around one-tenth of the baby's total body weight, compared to one-fiftieth in an adult.

In the first year after birth, the brain weight rockets to about 1,000 grams (35.2 ounces), two-thirds of its final adult size. Its growth then slows during infancy and childhood. This is also the main time for making new links or connections between nerve cells, as learning happens at an incredible speed. The brain's final growth spurt is during the teenage years, with full size reached at 14 to 16 years of age.

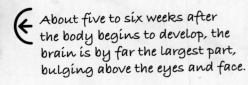
About five to six weeks after the body begins to develop, the brain is by far the largest part, bulging above the eyes and face.

Sex and the brain

The typical male brain is slightly larger than a female one, because a typical man is larger than an average woman. However, the female brain is bigger, compared to the size of the female body, than the male brain is compared to the male body.

There are few outer differences between a woman's brain and a man's. Recent research does show that the brains of females and males develop in different ways, even before birth. The differences are partly due to the effects of sex hormones. These are natural "messenger chemicals" made by the sex organs (ovaries in females, testes in males).

Even at birth, the brains of baby girls and baby boys have different "wiring diagrams." This allows each to become better at certain thinking tasks as they grow, although environment and upbringing can also have a great effect. Examples of differences are:

- Most women are better than most men at word-based tasks, such as remembering and recalling words from lists.
- Most men are better than most women at shape-based tasks, such as identifying objects seen from different angles.

Almost every day, a baby or young child learns new physical and mental skills—both based in the brain.

IN FOCUS: SEEING THE BRAIN

The brain can be seen or imaged by various types of medical machines and scanners:

- Computerized tomography (CT) and magnetic resonance (MR) scanners show small details of brain structure.

- Positron emission tomography (PET) scanners show which parts of the brain are using most energy; that is like showing the parts that are "thinking hardest."

- Cerebral arteriogram (angiogram) is a type of **X-ray** that reveals the blood vessels in the brain and shows if they are narrowed or blocked.

Brains in the Future

We know vast amounts about the brain—yet there is still so much more to learn. Research continues around the world, especially into the way that chemicals affect the brain. Some chemicals are recreational drugs that can devastate a person's intelligence and reason. Others are helpful medicines for problems, such as migraines, epilepsy, Parkinson's disease, and severe depression.

Behavior and psychology

The brain is the site of the mind. The workings of the mind—our mental activity—are studied by experts, such as psychologists and psychiatrists. There are many types and degrees of mental problems. Severe sadness or depression, extreme mood swings in manic depression, schizophrenia, autism, phobias (excessive unfounded fears), compulsive actions, obsessive desires, and addictive behavior are just a few. Some of these have a physical basis, perhaps caused by a brain tumor. Others are chemically based, possibly due to problems with "jumping" nerve signals from one nerve cell to the next. Other problems have no clear cause.

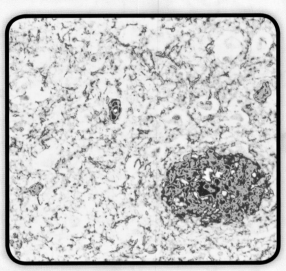

This colored light micrograph shows brain tissue from an Alzheimer sufferer. The diseased tissue is shown in blue.

The aging brain

Nerve cells are very specialized in their shapes and connections. After birth, they rarely multiply to produce new cells. From about the age of 20 years, the brain loses about 1 gram (0.03 ounces) in weight each year. This loss may speed up slightly in old age.

The aging brain may have reduced mental powers—or it may not. There is huge variation from person to person. In senile dementia, mental abilities are lost more rapidly than normal, from about the age of 60 or 70 years. There is usually failing memory (especially of recent events), anxiety, and difficulty with speech, expressing thoughts, and making sensible decisions.

In Alzheimer's disease, the changes of dementia occur earlier, perhaps from the age of 30 or 40 years. The brain itself shows signs of dead or "tangled" nerve cells. There are also objects, called plaques, around nerve cells, which disrupt their signals, and a lack of neurotransmitter chemicals.

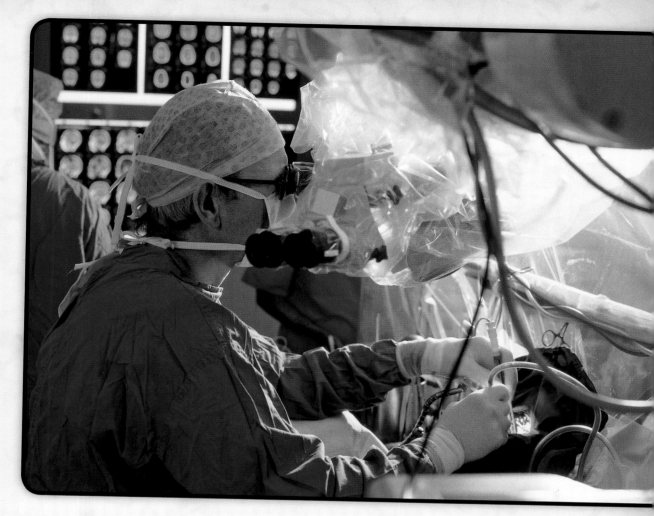

Future treatments

Medical treatments for brain problems improve every year. There are more effective drugs with fewer side effects, often designed using computers. Surgeons can operate on the microscopic level of individual nerve fibers. Substances called neural growth factors encourage damaged or cut nerve cells to repair or grow again.

A popularly held belief was that the adult brain could not make new nerve cells. However, it can, in parts such as the hippocampus and the olfactory (smell) areas. The new nerve cells are formed by stem cells. There are many kinds of research into the use of stem cells, gene therapy, neural growth factors, and similar treatments for various brain conditions.

 Through an operating microscope, the neurosurgeon can see and manipulate single nerve fibers.

IN FOCUS: ARE BIGGER BRAINS SMARTER?

There is no link between brain size and intelligence. On average, the size of the brains of people regarded as geniuses in their fields—science, philosophy, art, and sports—show no difference in size compared to the brains of ordinary people.

What Can Go Wrong with My Brain?

This book has explained the different parts of the brain, how they work, and how they may be damaged by injury and illness. The table below summarizes some of the problems that can affect young people. It also gives information about how each problem is treated and shows some of the ways you can prevent injury and illness.

Illness or injury	Cause	Symptoms	Prevention	Treatment
meningitis (several forms)	infection by germs (bacteria or viruses) spreading from elsewhere in body or through the air, or entering through a head wound or injury	depend on form, include headache, fever, stiff neck, nausea, vomiting, fear of bright light, dark skin rash, drowsiness, loss of consciousness	protect against head injury at all times, including wearing seat belts in vehicles, using protective equipment such as helmets in hazardous sports or pursuits	medical assessment, rest, medications such as antibiotics, depending on the type of germs
brain or head injury	severe physical shock, may cause bleeding (hemorrhage) in or around the brain, or skull fracture	pain, confusion, memory loss, headache, muscle weakness, numbness or tingling, temporary loss of consciousness (concussion) or longer-term unconsciousness	protect head at all times, including wearing seat belts in vehicles, using protective equipment such as helmets in hazardous sports or pursuits	urgent medical attention, especially after loss of consciousness (no matter how brief), even if the symptoms appear temporary, due to the risk of serious aftereffects
dyslexia (group of conditions that affect ability to read, write, and spell, and so affect general learning)	varied, including genetic influences, nerve development in an unborn baby's brain, nerve coordination of eyes and brain	problems with reading and perhaps writing, such as perceiving letters or words backwards—for example, "b" instead of "d," "on" instead of "no"	early recognition is extremely important, or the child may receive unsuitable help with learning	expert therapy as required, to improve reading, writing, and other skills
Bell's palsy	cranial nerve 7 (facial nerve) becomes swollen and pinched when it passes through and along the skull bone, perhaps due to viral infection	weakness and drooping of one side of the face, inability to close the eye or smile or make facial expressions. Taste may be affected.	no specific measures	steroid pills and perhaps antiviral medication
epilepsy	many forms of the condition. Some are linked to brain injury, damage, or tumor, or high body temperature, but many have no clear cause.	convulsions or seizures that recur, varying from short episodes of apparent "daydreaming," to random, jerky body movements, loss of muscle control, and unconsciousness	medical anti-convulsant drugs, mental techniques such as distraction, more rarely surgery	various kinds of anticonvulsant or anti-epileptic drugs (AEDs)

Many health problems can be avoided by simple, practical health measures, such as exercising regularly, getting plenty of rest, eating a balanced diet, being careful with high-risk activities, and having positive attitudes about dealing with stress and mental health.

Remember, if you think something is wrong with your body—or your mental state—you should always talk to a trained medical professional, like a doctor or a school nurse. Regular medical checkups are another important part of staying healthy, both in body and mind.

Find Out More

Books to read

Arnold, Nick. *Bulging Brains and Disgusting Digestion (Horrible Science)*. New York: Scholastic, 2009.

Ballard, Carol. *The Brain and Nervous System (Exploring the Human Body)*. Farmington Hills, Mich.: KidHaven, 2005.

Newquist, H. P. *The Great Brain Book: An Inside Look at the Inside of Your Head*. New York: Scholastic, 2004.

Parker, Steve. *Control Freak: Hormones, the Brain, and the Nervous System (Freestyle: Body Talk)*. Chicago: Raintree, 2007.

Websites to visit

www.tbiguide.com/howbrainworks.html
This is a straightforward, sensible site about memory, the brain, its parts, and how they work.

http://faculty.washington.edu/chudler/introb.html#bb
This "Neuroscience for Kids" site is about the brain, spinal cord, neurons, and the senses, with experiments, activities, and games.

Glossary

adrenaline neurotransmitter and a hormone substance that prepares the body for sudden physical action

aneurysm weak area, or balloon-like bulge or swelling

antibiotic type of medical drug that kills bacteria

auditory to do with hearing

autonomic able to work on its own or carry out actions by itself

axon long, thin part that carries signals away from a nerve cell body

bacteria group of microorganisms that can cause infections

biorhythm body process or condition that varies in a regular way, day and night

blood vessels network of tubes that carry blood around the body

cell microscopic unit or "building block" of a living thing. The body is made of trillions of cells.

cell body main part of a cell

cerebrum main dome-shaped upper part of the brain, consisting of two cerebral hemispheres

concussion short-term "blackout" or loss of consciousness

conscious being self-aware, alert, and able to respond to what is happening

convulsion movements, usually jerky and random, caused by uncontrolled pulling or contraction of muscles

cortex outer layer of a body part, such as the brain or kidney

cranial to do with the cranium, the dome-shaped upper skull

dendrite thin, branching part that carries nerve signals toward a nerve cell body

EEG electroencephalograph machine, which detects and displays the brain's tiny electrical nerve signals

epidemic widespread disease that occurs at a specific time

ganglia lump-like bulges, especially along nerves or in the brain

genetic to do with genes—the instructions for life and the genetic material, DNA

gland body part that makes and releases a product (usually a liquid), such as a hormone

gray matter part of the nervous system formed mainly of nerve cell bodies

hemorrhage leak of blood, bleeding

homeostasis keeping conditions inside the body constant and stable

hormone natural chemical substance that affects the workings of specific body parts

hypothalamus small part of the brain concerned with essential life functions, with close links to the hormonal system

inflammation swelling, redness, soreness, and perhaps pain

involuntary happening without the need for us to think or decide about it; something that we cannot control at will

ion tiny particle of a substance, such as a mineral, that is positive or negative

lobe name given to parts of the cerebrum of the brain

medulla inner layer of a body part, such as the brain or kidney

membrane sheet- or skin-like covering or lining layer

meninges three membranes wrapped around the brain and spinal cord

mental to do with thoughts and the mind

microbe very small living thing, only visible under a microscope

mineral one of a number of chemicals needed by the body in very small amounts—for example, calcium and iron

motor to do with muscles and the movements they make

myelin fatty substance wrapped around certain nerve fibers

neurotransmitter chemical substance that passes a nerve message from one nerve cell to the next, across the junction (synapse)

paralysis inability to move

peripheral around the edge, away from the middle or center

pituitary chief hormonal gland, just under the front of the brain

radiotherapy treatment involving radiation, such as X-rays or gamma rays

receptor place or site that receives or accepts a specific substance, like a lock that receives a key

REM sleep rapid eye movement sleep, a type of light or shallow sleep when dreams usually occur

sensory to do with detecting or sensing conditions, substances, or energy, like eyes sensing light rays

stem cell cell that has not become specialized but has the potential to develop into any kind of specialized cell, such as nerve cells, muscle cells, or blood cells

stress adverse, difficult, or challenging conditions, from physical fatigue or lack of food to emotional worry

synapse junction or join between two nerve cells, where they are separated by a tiny gap

tumor lump-like abnormal growth or swelling

ventricle fluid-filled chamber or cavity in a body part, such as the brain or heart

virus very small microorganism that can cause infection

white matter part of the nervous system formed mainly of nerve cell fibers

X-ray form of energy, as rays or radiation, that passes through soft body parts like flesh, but is stopped by hard parts, such as bones

Index